THE
INFOGRAPHIC
GUIDE TO
AMERICAN
GOVERNMENT

A VISUAL REFERENCE

FOR EVERYTHING YOU NEED TO KNOW

THE

INFOGRAPHIC

GUIDE TO

AMERICAN GOVERNMENT

CARISSA LYTLE and JARA KERN

Adams Media

New York London Toronto Sydney New Delhi

Adams Media
An Imprint of Simon & Schuster, Inc.
100 Technology Center Drive
Stoughton, Massachusetts 02072

First Adams Media trade paperback edition July 2019

ADAMS MEDIA and colophon are trademarks of Simon & Schuster.

For information about special discounts for bulk purchases, please contact Simon & Schuster Special Sales at 1-866-506-1949 or business@simonandschuster.com.

The Simon & Schuster Speakers Bureau can bring authors to your live event. For more information or to book an event contact the Simon & Schuster Speakers Bureau at 1-866-248-3049 or visit our website at www.simonspeakers.com.

Interior design by Carissa Lytle at Right Angle Studio, Inc.
Interior images © iStockphoto, Shutterstock, and Right Angle Studio, Inc.

Manufactured in China

10 9 8 7 6

ISBN 978-1-5072-1080-2
ISBN 978-1-5072-1081-9 (ebook)

Contains material adapted from the following title published by Adams Media, an Imprint of Simon & Schuster, Inc.: *American Government 101* by Kathleen Sears, copyright © 2016, ISBN 978-1-4405-9845-6.

CONTENTS

CHAPTER 1

HISTORY IN THE MAKING: THE FOUNDING OF THE AMERICAN GOVERNMENT

 The Enlightenment: A New Way of Thinking 14

 The Thirteen Colonies 16

 Resentment & Rebellion 18

 The American Revolution: What Was It About? 20

 Putting Will to the Quill: The Declaration of Independence 22

 The Revolutionary War: The Fight for Independence 24

Transitional Government: The Articles of Confederation 26

 Federalists vs. Anti-Federalists 28

 We the People: The First Six Articles of the Constitution 30

 The Race to Ratification 32

 Amendments to the Constitution 34

 Four Cornerstone Freedoms 36

 A Brief History of the Separation of Church & State 38

CHAPTER 2

THE ANATOMY OF THE AMERICAN GOVERNMENT

 The Three Branches **42**

 Checks & Balances: A New System for a New Country **44**

 All About the Senate **46**

 All About the House **48**

 Building a Law in Ten Steps **50**

 The Supreme Court: History and Powers **52**

 Did You Know?: Facts About Federal & State Courts **54**

 The Office of the President **56**

CHAPTER 3

DEMOCRACY IN ACTION: ELECTIONS & VOTING

 Ten Facts About Voting **60**

 Six Must-Knows About Campaigns & Elections **62**

 A Brief History of the Democratic Party **64**

 A Brief History of the Republican Party **66**

 Ten Facts on Third Parties & Independents **68**

 Red States, Blue States, & Swing States **70**

 What to Expect on Election Day **72**

 The Truth About Term Limits **74**

 Presidential Nominations & Elections **76**

 The Electoral College Explained **78**

 Winning the Electoral College but Losing the Popular Vote **80**

CHAPTER 4

THE PRESIDENT AND ADMINISTRATION LEADERSHIP

 Presidential Transitions: Eight Things to Know **84**

 The Inauguration: A Timeline **86**

 The Vice President: Duties & Selection **88**

 Next in Line: Presidential Succession at a Glance **90**

 All in a Day's Work **92**

 The Cabinet: What It Does and Who's in It **94**

 The First Lady **96**

 Impeachment: What? Why? When? How? **98**

 Keeping the Country Safe: National Security, Uncovered **100**

 The Civil Service **102**

CHAPTER 5

AMERICAN GOVERNMENT
MADE LOCAL

 State Government:
An Overview **106**

 Local Matters:
County Government **108**

 Community Matters:
City Government **110**

 A Free Press: Media
& the Government **112**

 All About Interest
Groups: Wielding
Influence Large and
Small **114**

 The Lowdown
on Lobbyists **116**

 What You Can Do:
Entering the Political
Process **118**

 Power of
the People **120**

The framers of the Constitution could not have foreseen the diversity and change that has swept through the United States since the Declaration of Independence in 1776. Yet they created a government that has kept the nation thriving and adaptive for more than two centuries, and set the precedent for many democracies around the world.

Of course, a system so large and detailed can be complex—and difficult to understand. That's where this book comes in: to organize and simplify the basic principles of American government, and explain them in fifty full-color, easy-to-understand spreads. With this guide, you'll learn about key aspects of American democracy, like the voting process in local, midterm, and presidential elections; how interest groups and lobbyists affect the government; and how the different branches of the political system function together. Entries will cover everything from the power of the free press to how the electoral college works to the basics of impeachment...and so much more!

Whether you're interested in the history of the US government, or in how the political system works today, *The Infographic Guide to American Government* illuminates everything you need or want to know about American government in a fun, illustrated format.

CHAPTER 1

HISTORY IN THE MAKING: THE FOUNDING OF THE AMERICAN GOVERNMENT

 The Enlightenment: A New Way of Thinking 14

 The Thirteen Colonies 16

 Resentment & Rebellion 18

 The American Revolution: What Was It About? 20

 Putting Will to the Quill: The Declaration of Independence 22

The Revolutionary War: The Fight for Independence 24

 Transitional Government: The Articles of Confederation 26

 Federalists vs. Anti-Federalists 28

 We the People: The First Six Articles of the Constitution 30

 The Race to Ratification 32

 Amendments to the Constitution 34

 Four Cornerstone Freedoms 36

 A Brief History of the Separation of Church & State 38

THE ENLIGHTENMENT:
A NEW WAY OF THINKING

Before the United States was a twinkle in the founding fathers' eyes, the ideals of the Enlightenment shaped a new way of thinking inspired by **freedom**, **democracy**, and **equality**.

MAJOR IDEAS & IDEALS:

> Freedom
> Liberty
> Justice
> Reason
> Scientific method

> Rejection of monarchy and aristocracy
> Skepticism of religion, especially the Catholic Church

THE AGE OF REASON

The Enlightenment was a philosophical movement in Europe and North America during the years 1685 to 1815. It sparked societal revolutions in England, America, and France.

PROMINENT THINKERS

Thomas Hobbes
Leviathan (1651)

John Locke
Second Treatise on Civil Government (1689)

Charles de Secondat, Baron de Montesquieu
The Spirit of the Laws (1748)

INFLUENCE ON AMERICA

Inspired by the ideas of prominent European thinkers, several early documents laid the foundation for a new government.

1620 Mayflower Compact—
any New World governing authority requires the consent of the people

1628 Petition of Right—
grants commoners a say in government

1689 English Bill of Rights—
grants certain rights to those accused of crimes, guarantees free elections

THE THIRTEEN COLONIES

The story of the American government begins with the earliest British settlements in North America.

───── ★ ─────

TYPES OF GOVERNMENT

Each colony fell into one of three categories:

CHARTER COLONIES

Governed by a legal document from Britain's crown

PROPRIETARY COLONIES

Governor appointed by the people who hold the charter for the colony

ROYAL COLONIES

Governor appointed by the king, local assembly of colonists

EARLY ARRIVALS

Roanoke Island, North Carolina, 1580s—*first colony, mysteriously abandoned*

Jamestown, Virginia, 1607—*first permanent settlement and trading outpost*

Plymouth, Massachusetts, 1620—*arrival of Pilgrims*

THE ORIGINAL THIRTEEN

By 1732, all thirteen colonies were established and flourishing in North America.

NEW YORK
1664

NEW HAMPSHIRE
1623

MASSACHUSETTS
1620

CONNECTICUT
1636

RHODE ISLAND
1636

PENNSYLVANIA
1681

NEW JERSEY
1664

MARYLAND
1632

DELAWARE
1664

VIRGINIA
1607

NORTH CAROLINA
1663

SOUTH CAROLINA
1663

GEORGIA
1732

HOME RULE

The colonies enjoyed home rule, or significant local autonomy, because of their distance from Britain. Several created early governing documents that resembled constitutions.

RESENTMENT & REBELLION

NO TAXATION WITHOUT REPRESENTATION

Colonists resented being taxed without having a say in their government. They embraced Enlightenment ideals and simmered with resentment over the sudden authority wielded by Britain. This opposition unified the colonists.

BOYCOTTS AND RISING TENSIONS

To protest taxation, colonists boycotted (refused to buy) British goods. These protests forced the British Parliament to repeal all taxes except a tax on tea. Yet through the 1760s and 1770s, tensions continued to rise.

During the **Era of Salutary Neglect** (1690–1763), relations between Britain and the colonies were smooth. Because of the vast distance between North America and Britain, the colonists had a great deal of freedom. Tensions began to rise in the 1760s with the levying of new taxes—a rise in tension which ultimately led to the American Revolution.

AN EMPTY TREASURY

After the seven-year French and Indian War, Britain was nearly bankrupt. To raise funds, Britain began to tax the colonies for the first time with laws, which included (among others):

1764 Sugar Act— taxed molasses, sugar, and other products

1764 Currency Act— made colonial currencies illegal, depressing colonial economy

1765 Quartering Act—forced colonists to host British soldiers

1765 Stamp Act—taxed newspapers, playing cards, and legal documents

1767 Townshend Acts— taxed lead, glass, tea, paper, and other items

★ THE ★
★ AMERICAN ★
★ REVOLUTION ★

WHAT WAS IT ABOUT?

Ultimately, the American Revolution was about independence, the dawn of a new way of thinking, and the colonists' desire to reject the authority of a faraway monarchy.

HERE'S HOW IT HAPPENED:

THE BOSTON TEA PARTY

To protest the tea tax and British rule, the Sons of Liberty (a secret organization of colonial patriots that fought against British taxation and rule) boarded three British ships in Boston Harbor in 1773 and dumped 342 chests of tea overboard.

SEIZING CONTROL

In response to the Boston Tea Party, King George III seized control of Boston's government; sent in troops and forced colonists to quarter them; and closed Boston Harbor.

FIRST CONTINENTAL CONGRESS

In 1774, colonists convened the First Continental Congress in Philadelphia, Pennsylvania, and wrote the Declaration of Rights with the goal of regaining home rule. They didn't.

HEATED DEBATES

Colonists were passionately divided on the right course of action forward.

FIRST ARMED CONFLICTS

By spring 1775, fighting between the British army and the colonists was already underway.

"It is infinitely wiser and safer, to form a constitution of our own in a cool deliberate manner, while we have it in our power, than to trust such an interesting event to time and chance."

– THOMAS PAINE, *COMMON SENSE*

COMMON SENSE

Thomas Paine's 1776 pamphlet *Common Sense* clarified the revolutionary cause. Within a few months, more than 120,000 copies had been sold.

PUTTING WILL TO THE QUILL

THE DECLARATION OF INDEPENDENCE

With tensions continuing to rise and fighting already underway, the Americans formally declared independence from Britain in a document known as the **Declaration of Independence**.

WHO?

Thomas Jefferson—who would become the United States' third president—drafted the Declaration and presented it to the full Second Continental Congress in **Philadelphia** in **late June 1776**.

 WHEN?

WHERE?

4TH OF JULY

Americans celebrate July 4, **Independence Day**, as a national holiday because it's the date that Congress formally adopted the Declaration.

FUN FACT

The document received most of its iconic signatures on **August 2** because of a delay in printing 200 copies.

A LANDMARK DOCUMENT

The Declaration changed the course of human events by putting forth:

NEW GOVERNING PRINCIPLES
For a government in which all persons are created equal with certain unalienable rights and where power is derived from the consent of the governed

GRIEVANCES
Specific problems Americans had with King George III

DECLARATION
Formal statement of the colonies' independence

THE REVOLUTIONARY WAR

★ ★ ★ THE FIGHT FOR INDEPENDENCE ★ ★ ★

1775

» Paul Revere and William Dawes warn "the British are coming"

» Minutemen and colonists clash at Lexington and Concord

» Second Continental Congress

» George Washington named commander in chief

» Battle of Bunker Hill

» Failed invasion of Canada by General Benedict Arnold and General Richard Montgomery

1776

» Thomas Paine's *Common Sense* published

» Redcoats defeat Americans in the Battle of Long Island

» British occupy New York City

» Washington crosses the Delaware River to attack British troops stationed in Trenton, New Jersey

THE WAR WASN'T EASY TO WIN —
BRITAIN WAS A MAJOR WORLD POWER ON LAND
AND SEA. GRIT, DETERMINATION, WEATHER,
AND A JUST-IN-TIME ALLIANCE MADE THE
AMERICANS VICTORIOUS BY LATE 1781.

1777

» Americans are victorious in Connecticut and Vermont

» British occupy Philadelphia and claim Pennsylvania

1778

» France signs on as an American ally

» British occupy Georgia, but abandon Philadelphia

1779

» British defeated in South Carolina, Georgia, and in the Western theater

» Spain declares war on Britain

» Britain burns swaths of Connecticut

1780

» Battles for the South rock North and South Carolina

1781

» Battles for the South continue

» French drive the British from Chesapeake Bay

» Articles of Confederation ratified by all thirteen states

» Britain's General Charles Cornwallis, surrounded on land and sea, surrenders in Yorktown, Virginia, on October 19

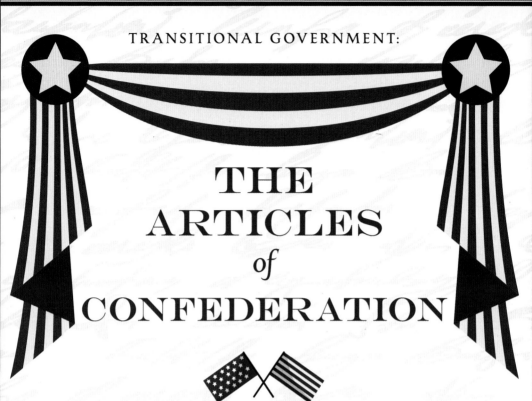

THE ARTICLES *of* CONFEDERATION

Revolutionary leaders were wary of creating a new and powerful central government. The Articles established a loose confederation of independent states with the authority of local rule.

WHEN?

Authored in 1776

Ratified 1778–1781

WHY?

The Articles of Confederation was the colonists' first attempt to create a new form of government.

WHAT IT ESTABLISHED:

Single-body (unicameral)
Congress with limited power

One vote per state

No independent executive
or judiciary branch

Unanimous approval for major legislation
and amendments, which gave single states
veto power over the central government

WHAT IT FAILED TO ESTABLISH:

National currency

Treaty enforcement

Revenue through taxation

Peace between the states

LESSONS LEARNED:

Served as a transitional government
between the revolutionary period and
the birth of the modern republic

Proved a "government
of consent" could work

Gave the United States its name

FEDERALISTS VS.

AND THE SQUABBLE

WHAT'S THE DIFFERENCE?

FEDERALISTS

Federalists believed in the importance of a strong central government sharing power with the states

PROMINENT FEDERALISTS:

James Madison

Alexander Hamilton

John Jay

ANTI-FEDERALISTS

Suspicious of central government, the Anti-Federalists preferred direct democracy and local rule

PROMINENT ANTI-FEDERALISTS:

Patrick Henry

John Hancock

Samuel Adams

James Monroe

ANTI-FEDERALISTS

OVER STATES' RIGHTS

After the Articles of Confederation failed, it was clear that the new government required a careful balance between state and national power. The drafting of a new constitution began with the Constitutional Convention in 1787.

At the heart of the divide was the question of where power should lie.

THE FEDERALIST PAPERS

In 1787, both sides began to publish essays to build support for their causes. Madison, Hamilton, and Jay's collection of essays—*The Federalist Papers*—became the definitive argument in favor of the new American Constitution.

> "
> *The operations of the federal government will be most extensive and important in times of war and danger; those of the State governments, in times of peace and security.*"
>
> —James Madison, *The Federalist Papers*

We the People

THE FIRST SIX ARTICLES

OF

THE CONSTITUTION

Article 1

- Established the legislative branch

- Created a two-chamber Congress with a House of Representatives and a Senate

- Outlined the chambers' operating procedures and powers

Article 2

- Established the executive branch

- Defined the powers of the presidency

- Created the method of electing the president— the Electoral College

Article 3

- Established the judicial branch of government and the federal court system

During the summer of 1787, delegates from all states (except Rhode Island*) met at the Constitutional Convention in Philadelphia, Pennsylvania, to hammer out a new set of governing principles. The result was the Constitution.

Article 4

- Dictated the relationship between the states

- Distributed political authority between federal and state governments

Article 5

- Outlined how amendments—or changes—to the Constitution must be made:

- $2/3$ vote by each chamber of Congress, ratification by ¾ of state legislatures

- Second Constitutional Convention (never used)

Article 6

- Declared federal laws take precedence over state laws

- Required every federal and state official to pledge to uphold the Constitution

*Rhode Island skipped the Constitutional Convention out of fear it would create a new set of laws giving the government too much power–exactly what ended up happening!

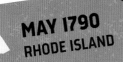

MAY 1790
RHODE ISLAND

NOVEMBER 1789
NORTH CAROLINA

JULY 1788
NEW YORK

JUNE 1788
NEW HAMPSHIRE | VIRGINIA

THE RACE TO RATIFICATION

In the winter of 1787, state conventions began to ratify the Constitution.

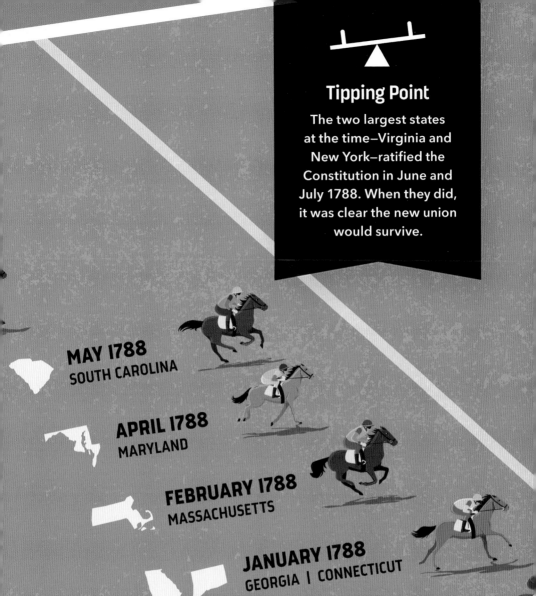

Tipping Point

The two largest states at the time—Virginia and New York—ratified the Constitution in June and July 1788. When they did, it was clear the new union would survive.

MAY 1788
SOUTH CAROLINA

APRIL 1788
MARYLAND

FEBRUARY 1788
MASSACHUSETTS

JANUARY 1788
GEORGIA | CONNECTICUT

DECEMBER 1787
DELAWARE | PENNSYLVANIA
NEW JERSEY

AMENDMENTS
to the Constitution

The authors of the constitution made

amendments (changes) difficult because they

wanted the core of the document to

remain the same. They were confident

that they had created a government

that would stand the test of time,

however, they did recognize the need

for amendments. then and in the future

What Is an Amendment?

An amendment is a change to the Constitution. Amendments are either proposed by two-thirds of all the members in the House and Senate, or by a convention that two-thirds of the states call for. For the amendment to be ratified (approved/validated), it then must be voted for by three-quarters of state legislatures, (38 out of 50 states), or by three-quarters of the states through a special ratification convention.

Bill of Rights

‣ First ten amendments to the Constitution

‣ Created in 1789, ratified in 1791

‣ Guaranteed personal freedoms and rights, including the freedoms of speech and religion

‣ Limited government's power

‣ Gave powers not delegated to Congress to the states or the people

RUNNING THE NUMBERS

11,699
total proposals—
and counting

200 amendments
introduced during
each two-year
congressional term

27 total amendments,
including Bill of Rights

1992:
the 27th Amendment, the most recent, requires a $^2/_3$ majority vote for Congress to give its members raises

1 amendment
repealed: the 21st Amendment in 1933 repealed the 18th Amendment, ending Prohibition

Amendments include:

‣ Abolition of slavery
‣ Clarification of citizenship
‣ Presidential term limits
‣ Voting age
‣ Women's right to vote

FREEDOM OF RELIGION

Prohibits laws that interfere with religious beliefs or opinions

Allows laws that regulate or ban certain religious practices (for instance, human sacrifice)

RIGHT TO PETITION & ASSEMBLY

Protects the right to petition the government on grievances

Allows the right to assemble peacefully to express dissent

FREEDOM OF SPEECH & THE PRESS

Guarantees the right to the freedom of personal expression

Protects freedom of the press—now broadly interpreted as the media

CORNERSTONE FREEDOMS

The Bill of Rights—especially the 1st Amendment—protects some of Americans' most cherished freedoms. The framers of the Constitution believed these freedoms were the cornerstones of democracy.

RIGHT TO BEAR ARMS

Protects the right to keep and bear arms for personal defense

A BRIEF HISTORY
OF THE SEPARATION OF
CHURCH & STATE

The concept of the separation of church and state defines the distance between organized religion and the government.

EARLY THINKER: JOHN LOCKE (1632–1704)

This Enlightenment philosopher argued that the government could not rule the individual conscience. He also promoted religious tolerance. His views influenced the drafting of the Constitution.

THE 1ST AMENDMENT

The 1st Amendment prevents the government from:

- Creating an official national religion
- Prohibiting any practice of religion

THE BAPTISTS

In the late 1790s, Baptists living in Anglican Virginia sought religious tolerance. They thought government limitations against religion were wrong.

THOMAS JEFFERSON

In 1802, as president, Jefferson wrote to the Baptists that the Bill of Rights prevented the establishment of a national church and that citizens did not have to fear government influence in the practice of religion.

CHAPTER 2

THE ANATOMY OF THE AMERICAN GOVERNMENT

 The Three Branches **42**

 Checks & Balances: A New System for a New Country **44**

 All About the Senate **46**

 All About the House **48**

 Building a Law in Ten Steps **50**

 The Supreme Court: History and Powers **52**

 Did You Know?: Facts About Federal & State Courts **54**

 The Office of the President **56**

THE THREE BRANCHES

The US federal government, as well as all state governments, has three branches—the legislative, the executive, and the judicial—each of which performs specific functions.

LEGISLATIVE
CONGRESS

The legislative branch consists of the Senate and the House of Representatives—known collectively as Congress.

- Creates and passes laws
- Creates and manages the federal government's budget
- Legislators are elected by the people

Did You Know?

Sixteen senators have been elected to serve as president, but **only three** have been elected directly from the Senate to the White House. The most recent was Barack Obama in 2008.

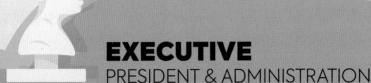

EXECUTIVE
PRESIDENT & ADMINISTRATION

The executive branch includes the president, vice president, fifteen cabinet-level departments, and dozens of agencies, such as NASA. The president chooses the vice president and appoints cabinet members.

- Facilitates day-to-day federal government responsibilities
- Oversees armed forces
- Represents US foreign, domestic, and economic interests
- Over a million people work for the federal government, not counting the armed forces

JUDICIAL
THE COURTS

Consisting of the US Supreme Court and lower federal courts, the judicial branch decides cases and the constitutionality of laws.

- Hears cases that challenge constitutionality or require interpretation of legislation
- Decides cases involving laws and treaties
- Resolves disputes between states

CHECKS & BALANCES

A NEW SYSTEM FOR A NEW COUNTRY

3
BRANCHES IN ACTION

EXECUTIVE
President

LEGISLATIVE
Congress

JUDICIAL
Supreme Court

- The president can veto laws passed by Congress.

- Congress can override a presidential veto with a $\frac{2}{3}$ majority.

- Congress, with a $\frac{2}{3}$ majority vote in both the House and Senate, can propose amendments to the Constitution. These must be ratified by $\frac{3}{4}$ of the states.

- The Supreme Court can determine the constitutionality of laws.

THE FRAMERS OF THE CONSTITUTION HAD NO DESIRE TO RETURN TO THE SYSTEM OF DESPOTIC RULE THEY HAD LIVED UNDER IN COLONIAL AMERICA. THEY CAREFULLY ESTABLISHED A GOVERNMENT BASED ON THE SEPARATION OF POWERS.

WHY?

- **Prevents the concentration of power** by forcing each branch to share authority
- **Limits any one branch** from becoming supreme
- **Defines the functions** of each
- **Creates checks and balances** to counteract autocracy

Older Ideals

The concept of a three-branch government was not new. In ancient Greece, Aristotle wrote about mixed government. During the Enlightenment, French philosopher Baron de Montesquieu wrote about the "distribution of powers" in his 1748 treatise *The Spirit of the Laws*.

HOW?

The federal government and state governments were divided, and each was subdivided into branches. Each branch has separate and independent powers and areas of responsibility.

 **Did You Know?**

There have been twenty-seven amendments to the Constitution since 1789. Seven of them can be considered to supersede Supreme Court rulings. For example, the 13th and 14th Amendments were responses to *Dred Scott v. Sandford* (1857), which stated that slaves and their descendants could never be citizens.

ALL ABOUT

THE SENATE

The Senate is considered the "upper" or "elite" house of Congress. Each state elects two senators, no matter how many people live within its borders.

NUMBER OF SENATORS:

100 2 FROM EACH STATE

TERM LENGTH:

6 YEARS

1913

The year citizens began directly electing their senators. Until then, senators were selected by state legislatures.

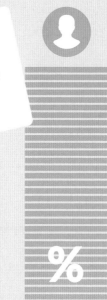

TIEBREAKER:

The vice president, who casts the deciding vote when senators are split 50/50.

ELIGIBILITY:

✔ **Minimum age:** thirty years old.

✔ **A resident** of the state they would represent.

✔ **Years as a citizen:** nine or more.

SPECIAL POWERS:

- The president's judicial and cabinet-level appointees must first be approved by the Senate.

- The Senate is responsible for ratifying treaties.

- If the president is impeached in the House, the trial is held in the US Senate. A two-thirds vote of the Senate is required to convict the president, something that has never happened.

ALL ABOUT

THE HOUSE

The other house of Congress is called the House of Representatives. It is sometimes referred to as "the People's House" because members represent the smallest unit of the population.

RULES RULE

The House is ruled by a strict hierarchy, and much of the actual work of the House is done in committees—standing committees such as Agriculture, Budget, and Energy and Commerce; special committees for investigations; and joint committees between the House and Senate.

SPECIAL POWERS:

- All revenue bills must originate in the House.

- The House is charged with impeaching the president for "high crimes and misdemeanors."

- The House elects the president in the case of an Electoral College tie.

435*

NUMBER OF REPRESENTATIVES

747,184

AVERAGE NUMBER OF CITIZENS REPRESENTED BY A HOUSE MEMBER

 *As of 2018, House seats are assigned to states based on **population levels**, which are revised every ten years with the US Census. Each state has at least one House member. Currently, California has the greatest number—fifty-three.

ELIGIBILITY:

✓ **Minimum age:** twenty-five years old.

✓ **A resident** of the state they would represent.

✓ **Years as a citizen:** seven or more.

TERM LENGTH:

2 YEARS

BUILDING A LAW IN TEN STEPS

Hundreds of national laws are passed each year. The framers of the Constitution created a process that makes it tremendously difficult for laws to be created in order to prevent them from overreaching. Here's how it works.

STEP 1
A bill is introduced
A bill can be inspired by anything or anyone, but only a member of Congress can sponsor it.

STEP 2
Legislation is drafted
Words are put to paper and the sponsor builds support with other legislators.

STEP 3
Committee review
At least one House committee reviews the bill.

STEP 4
Hearings take place
Opinions are voiced, support coalesces, or media attention builds.

STEP 5
Markup & submission
This phase includes language revisions, amendments, and the final vote.

STEP 7
Floor action
The bill must receive 218 votes in the House to go to the floor.

STEP 8
Voting
Members of Congress have only three choices: yes, no, or present. "Present" is used to abstain.

STEP 9
Agreement
Before it goes to the president, the House and Senate versions must be identical.

STEP 6
Calendaring
Before heading to the floor, bills must be put on the House and Senate calendars—which is easier said than done. Each chamber has specific calendars that determine the order in which bills are taken up. Between the House and Senate, there are six calendars in all!

STEP 10
Signed or vetoed
The president then signs a bill into law—or vetoes it. If it's vetoed, the House and Senate can override the veto, but doing so requires a ⅔ majority vote in both chambers.

THE SUPREME COURT:

PURPOSE
The Supreme Court interprets the Constitution and determines the constitutionality of laws.

80-100
Number of cases heard each year.

IN SESSION
First Monday in October to late June or early July.

APPOINTMENT FOR LIFE
Justices are appointed by the president. They serve until they die or retire. The president chooses justices on the basis of ideology, confirmability, age, race, and gender. All appointees must be confirmed by a two-thirds majority vote in the Senate.

REQUIREMENTS
While there are no age or citizenship requirements, by tradition, all justices have been **trained in the law**, and have been **American citizens over the age of thirty**.

HISTORY AND POWERS

BROAD VS. NARROW

Over the last two centuries, the Supreme Court has sometimes broadly and sometimes narrowly interpreted the Constitution. Its rulings have given the federal government the ability to regulate commerce and the economy, expanded citizens' civil rights, and curtailed citizens' rights to privacy.

TRIAL COURT & APPELLATE JURISDICTION

The Supreme Court hears:

- Trial cases, such as cases between the states or those arising under treaties
- Cases already decided by a lower federal court or a state court

DID YOU KNOW?

The Supreme Court can occasionally overturn its own rulings. *Plessy v. Ferguson* (1896) entrenched the idea of "separate but equal" facilities for whites and blacks. *Brown v. Board of Education* (1954) overturned it.

DID YOU KNOW?

Think about the federal court system as a pyramid, with the Supreme Court on top, the appellate courts in the middle, and the district courts at the bottom. The separate, independent state court systems have the same structure.

1789

The year in which the **Judiciary Act** established the **three-part court system**

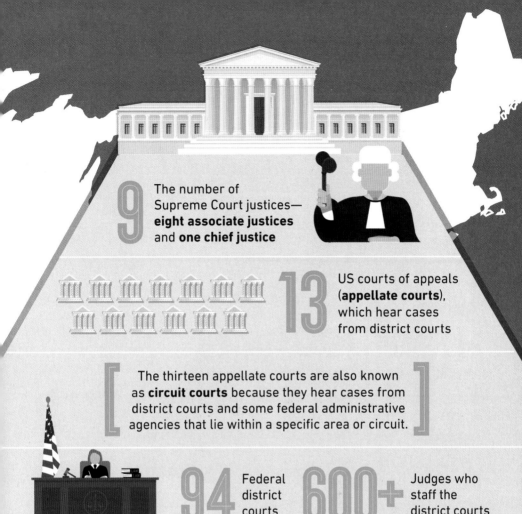

9 The number of Supreme Court justices—**eight associate justices** and **one chief justice**

13 US courts of appeals (**appellate courts**), which hear cases from district courts

[The thirteen appellate courts are also known as **circuit courts** because they hear cases from district courts and some federal administrative agencies that lie within a specific area or circuit.]

94 Federal district courts

600+ Judges who staff the district courts

Federal Decisions
Cases between the states, involving the government, concerning bankruptcy, or decisions on appeals.

State Decisions
Cases on felonies and misdemeanors, business and real estate disputes, divorce and custody suits, personal injury lawsuits, and other matters between individuals.

Judicial Review
Process by which laws are declared constitutional or unconstitutional by the courts.

Court of Last Resort
Each state has a court of last resort that serves as the final arbiter of state law. While most of them are state supreme courts, New York calls its court of last resort the "court of appeals."

THE OFFICE OF THE PRESIDENT

While the framers of the Constitution established Congress as the first branch of government, the presidency has been the focal point of the American governmental system for more than two hundred years.

NATIONALLY ELECTED

The president and vice president run together and are the only nationally elected offices. The candidate who wins election is the president of all the people.

"MR. PRESIDENT"

George Washington's choice for formal address has endured since he held office.

MANY ROLES. ONE OFFICE.

The president represents American ideals and aspirations—both at home and abroad.

Commander in Chief

Chief Executive

Head of State

Chief Legislator

Chief Diplomat

ELIGIBILITY

Article 2 of the Constitution states the president must:

- Be a **natural-born** citizen
- Be at least **thirty-five** years of age at inauguration
- Have **fourteen** or more years as a US resident

TERM LIMITS

- Two four-year terms
- Only term-limited position in the three government branches

GEORGE WASHINGTON

The first American president was careful to set the tone for future presidencies. He voluntarily walked away from the presidency after two terms, turning over national power to someone else.

CHAPTER 3

DEMOCRACY IN ACTION: ELECTIONS & VOTING

 Ten Facts About Voting **60**

 Six Must-Knows About Campaigns & Elections **62**

 A Brief History of the Democratic Party **64**

 A Brief History of the Republican Party **66**

 Ten Facts on Third Parties & Independents **68**

 Red States, Blue States, & Swing States **70**

 What to Expect on Election Day **72**

 The Truth About Term Limits **74**

 Presidential Nominations & Elections **76**

 The Electoral College Explained **78**

 Winning the Electoral College but Losing the Popular Vote **80**

A CORNERSTONE OF AMERICAN DEMOCRACY, THE RIGHT TO VOTE IS AMONG CITIZENS' MOST FUNDAMENTAL.

TEN FACTS
ABOUT VOTING

1 ENFRANCHISEMENT/SUFFRAGE: The right to vote.

2 A government where power is bestowed by the ballot box, not hereditary inheritance? **That was revolutionary in 1776.** Only white Protestant males who owned property, however, could cast a ballot.

3 Only 6% of the population was eligible to vote in the **first presidential election**.

7 Only **American citizens** are eligible to vote.

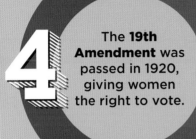

4 The **19th Amendment** was passed in 1920, giving women the right to vote.

Passage of the **24th Amendment** and the Voting Rights Act of 1965 gave African Americans full enfranchisement.

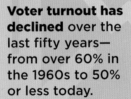

9 **Voter turnout has declined** over the last fifty years—from over 60% in the 1960s to 50% or less today.

5 Minimum voting age (eighteen) was established when the **26th Amendment** was ratified in 1971.

6 Depending on what state they live in, voters can vote **in person, by mail, or as an absentee**.

10 The "Motor Voter Act" or **National Voter Registration Act** of 1993 allows citizens to register to vote when applying for a driver's license.

BALLOT

SIX

MUST-KNOWS ABOUT CAMPAIGNS & ELECTIONS

Running for elected office demands a dizzying array of administrative and campaign duties.

1 ELECTION DAY

The general election is held in November on the first Tuesday after the first Monday, or the first Tuesday after November 1. Elections have been held as early as November 2 and as late as November 8.

NOVEMBER

Sun	Mon	Tue	Wed	Thu	Fri	Sat
	1	2	3	4	5	6
7	8	9	10	11	12	13
14	15	16	17	18	19	20
21	22	23	24	25	26	27
28	29	30				

2 PRESIDENTIAL ELECTIONS

Held every

★ ★ 4 YEARS ★ ★

3 MIDTERMS

Congressional elections held halfway through a presidential term.

④ BALLOT ACCESS

A ballot is what voters use to cast a vote, and ballot access refers to the regulations under which a candidate can appear on the ballot. Ballot rules are particular to each state as well as to eligibility—citizenship, age, residency, and so forth.

⑤ NOMINATIONS

The winner of the primary election or season emerges as the party's nominee. In the presidential race, each major party formally selects a nominee at its summer convention.

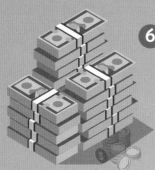

⑥ HOW MUCH DOES IT COST?

It is expensive to run for office:

- President—general election: **$1 BILLION**
- Senate seat: **$10.4 MILLION**
- House seat: **$1.3 MILLION**

DID YOU KNOW?

What is gerrymandering? Sometimes, voting districts are redrawn to benefit one political party over another. This practice is called gerrymandering. The name comes from Elbridge Gerry, the fifth US vice president, who first signed the practice into law in 1812 as governor of Massachusetts.

A BRIEF HISTORY
OF THE
DEMOCRATIC PARTY

★ 19 ★

Number of **Democratic presidents** from 1800 to 2016.

1ST PARTY PRESIDENT

Thomas Jefferson, elected in 1800.

The country's two-party system has its origins in the squabbles over **state vs. federal power** during the Constitution's ratification.

Who Were the Democratic-Republicans?

Federalists believed in the supremacy of central government. Opponents favoring **states' rights** formed the Democratic-Republican Party.

Early Platform and Dominance

They supported an **agrarian-based economy** favoring farmers and tradesmen, and successfully organized at the local and state levels to become the dominant party early on.

Splinter

After a **contentious 1824 Electoral College election**, the Democratic-Republicans became the Democrats and the Republicans reorganized as the Whigs.

Modern Party

Today, the Democratic Party is further to the left and known as the more liberal of the two major parties, favoring bigger government and more expansive social policies.

A BRIEF HISTORY OF THE

REPUBLICAN PARTY

1ST PARTY PRESIDENT

Abraham Lincoln, elected in 1860.

★ 19 ★

Number of **Republican presidents** from 1800 to 2016.

The Republican Party was founded just before the Civil War and became ascendant during the war itself.

Early Platform

The anti-slavery stance of the Republican Party **infuriated the Southern states**, contributing to their secession and the Civil War.

GOP

"Grand Old Party," the nickname for the Republican Party, was first used in 1875.

Dominance from 1860–1932

Republicans dominated Congress and the presidency, becoming known as the party of "big business" in the early twentieth century.

Modern Party

The Republican Party is **further to the right**—more conservative—than the Democratic Party in both its approach to government's size and influence, and its stance on social issues.

TEN

FACTS ON

THIRD PARTIES & INDEPENDENTS

The two-party system sets American government apart from most other democracies, which have parliamentary systems featuring multiparty elections and legislative bodies.

1 A two-party history

American government has been a two-party system since its creation.

2 Proportional representation

In other democracies, this is an alternate apportionment in which parties are represented in the legislature by the percentage of the vote they won.

3 Winner-takes-all system

The candidate who receives the most votes is the one who takes office.

4 Difficulty

Traditionally it has been difficult for third parties to gain traction with voters.

5 Few elected officials

Third-party candidates win very few state or national offices. The most famous example is Senator Bernie Sanders of Vermont, who is the longest-serving Independent member of Congress in American history.

6 No third-party presidents

All American presidents have been major-party nominees.

7 Green Party

"Greens" believe corporations exploit American interests for gain and support radical social and economic reform.

8 Issue duality

Candidates and voters tend to see only two sides to major issues.

9 Libertarian Party

Libertarians support extremely limited government and believe its power should be used to protect the country's borders and maintain civil order.

10 Reform Party

Founded in 1995 by Henry Ross Perot in his bid for the presidency, the centrist Reform Party frayed by 2015.

RED STATES, BLUE STATES, & SWING STATES

The terms **"red states"** and **"blue states"** refer to states whose voters predominantly choose Republican or Democratic presidential candidates, respectively. **"Swing states"** are harder to predict and often determine the outcome of the Electoral College vote.

DID YOU KNOW?

Many people assume that the red and blue designations have been around since the country's founding, but this dichotomy is much more recent. During the weeks prior to the 2000 presidential election, major news networks designated blue for Democratic state wins and red for Republican wins.

RED STATES

- ▸ "Safe" states for **Republican** candidates
- ▸ Perceived as **conservative**
- ▸ Strongholds in the **Deep South** and the country's more **rural interior**

BLUE STATES

- ▸ "Safe" states for **Democratic** candidates
- ▸ Perceived as **liberal**
- ▸ Often includes the **West Coast**, **upper East Coast**, and areas with heavy **urban populations**

SWING STATES

- ▸ States in which **both major-party** candidates receive strong support
- ▸ Typically **determine the outcome** of presidential elections
- ▸ Sometimes also referred to as **"purple states"** or **"battleground states"**
- ▸ Include areas of the **Midwest**, **Mountain West**, **Mid-Atlantic**, and **Southwest**

WHEN SWING STATES STOP SWINGING

Gradual demographic changes over the course of several election cycles can shift a state **from "swing" to "red" or "blue" status**. For instance, Ohio has been shifting more reliably toward a red state, while Colorado has moved toward blue.

While primaries and caucuses may take place on different dates in different states, Election Day is always the Tuesday after the first Monday in November. **Here is how the run-up and day-of work.**

NOVEMBER

6

WHAT TO EXPECT ON ELECTION DAY

DID YOU KNOW?

In November 1948, incumbent Harry S. Truman beat challenger Thomas E. Dewey in an upset victory. The *Chicago Tribune*, eager to be the first to "call" the election, printed the now-famous "Dewey Defeats Truman" headline—too early!

TURNOUT

Each party focuses on turning out its base in early voting and on Election Day itself.

VOTER POLLING

Before and during Election Days, professional pollsters take daily tracking polls to determine how close the race is—at all levels, from national to local.

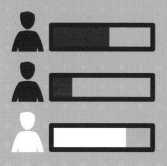

DETERMINING OUTCOMES

Polls close at different times in each state and time zone. Once they have closed, election workers tally the results and report them when it becomes clear that a candidate has won. Results are reported in online, TV, and print news, as well as on candidates' websites and social media. In the presidential election, **once a candidate garners 270 projected electoral votes, the election is "called" for the winner** by the Associated Press and other news organizations.

THE TRUTH ABOUT TERM LIMITS

HISTORY

Term limits date back to antiquity. In the US, they were first introduced in the Articles of Confederation in 1781 to limit the number of years delegates could serve.

A term limit legally restricts the number of terms an elected official can serve. They apply to offices at the state and federal levels.

Passionate arguments for and against term limits were part of the Constitutional Convention in 1787 but were not included in the original Constitution itself.

Presidential Term Limits

Term limits on the American presidency were not established until 1951—well after Franklin Delano Roosevelt had served a partial fourth term until his death in 1945. The 22nd Amendment limits the president to **two elected terms,** or a total time of **no more than ten years** in the case of a VP ascending to the office.

Gubernatorial Term Limits

In thirty-six states, the governor is limited to **no more than two consecutive terms** or no more than two lifetime terms—or about eight years of service in office.

Legislative Term Limits

While there are no term limits on members of Congress, fifteen state legislatures have imposed term limits ranging **from eight to sixteen years** of total time in office.

Municipal Term Limits

Certain municipal roles come with term limits. The mayorships of Philadelphia, Houston, New York City, and Los Angeles, have term limits. City council positions in many municipalities also come with **a range of term limits.**

PRESIDENTIAL NOMINATIONS & ELECTIONS

Presidential elections are held every four years and are a massive undertaking for any serious candidate.

Here's how the process works.

Organizing a Campaign

Candidates need enormous political networks. Long before the general election, they:

- ‣ Begin raising money
- ‣ Establish contacts with the media
- ‣ Create a network of supporters

Raising Money

Running for president costs serious money, so candidates and key supporters focus on raising campaign "war chests."

- ‣ **$50-100 million** to organize campaign
- ‣ **$70 million+** for general election

Primaries and Caucuses

In primary elections and caucuses, registered voters cast ballots to select which candidate will run as the party's nominee in the general election. They're held for presidential elections as well as for a variety of national, state, and local elections.

- **Open Primary:** Voters do not need to claim a party affiliation to vote; they can vote in the Republican or the Democratic primary, no matter which party they are registered under.

- **Closed Primary:** Voters need to declare their party affiliation in order to vote; only registered Republicans can vote for Republicans in a closed primary, and the same for Democrats.

- **Jungle Primary:** All candidates in the primary run against each other and are not divided by parties. The top two winners are then the candidates for that election.

Prominent primaries and caucuses include:

- Iowa caucus
- New Hampshire primary
- Super Tuesday primaries and caucuses

Debates and Forums

A year before the primaries, public debates give candidates the opportunity to build momentum—and voters the chance to compare them.

Nomination

The official nominations take place at each party's summer convention.

THE ELECTORAL COLLEGE
— EXPLAINED —

The president and vice president are actually elected by the Electoral College. Why? The framers of the Constitution feared direct democracy and wanted to protect the interests of the states. For these reasons, they devised a layered election system.

ELECTORS

Voters select the president and vice president, but they actually choose a slate of electors who cast the official vote. Voters cast ballots for their preferred candidates for president, and electors pledged to the winning candidate then meet in their state capital to cast their ballots, which reflect the will of the voters in that state. These results are then sent to Congress, which opens and counts the ballots in January.

538

The number of Electoral College votes:

- ▶ **435** for the House
- ▶ **100** for the Senate
- ▶ **3** for the District of Columbia

270

The number of Electoral College votes needed to win.

WINNER TAKES ALL...MOSTLY

The candidate who wins the majority of the vote in a state takes all its Electoral College votes.

MAINE & NEBRASKA

The only two states that can split their Electoral College votes.

OFFICIAL VOTE

The presidential election takes place in November, but the electors meet in December to cast the official vote.

CALLS FOR REFORM

Eliminating or reforming the Electoral College would take a constitutional amendment approved by two-thirds of both the House and Senate and ratified by three-quarters of the states. With so many congressional members from smaller, rural areas that favor this system, passage would be tremendously difficult.

DID YOU KNOW?

5 The number of presidents who won the Electoral College but lost the popular vote.

WINNING THE ELECTORAL COLLEGE

BUT

LOSING THE POPULAR VOTE

Thanks to the Electoral College, it is possible to win the presidency while losing the popular vote.

TIEBREAKER

It's technically possible for both candidates to win 270 electoral votes. If this happens, the election is decided by the House of Representatives.

WHY?

The Constitution and the establishment of the Electoral College **preserved the rights of the states—and the importance of the less-populated areas of the country**. Despite the density of the country's urban centers, candidates can't ignore large areas of its interior in their quest for the magic 270 votes.

HOW?

If more voters cast ballots for one candidate, but they're disproportionately located in the urban areas of the West and East coasts, **it's certainly possible to garner more overall votes,** despite not racking up 270 electoral votes.

WHEN?

	Popular Vote Winner	Presidential Winner	Margin
1824	Andrew Jackson	John Quincy Adams	40,000+
1876	Samuel J. Tilden	Rutherford B. Hayes	254,000+
1888	Grover Cleveland	Benjamin Harrison	90,000+
2000	Al Gore	George W. Bush	544,000
2016	Hillary Clinton	Donald J. Trump	2.3 million

CHAPTER 4

THE PRESIDENT AND ADMINISTRATION LEADERSHIP

 Presidential Transitions: Eight Things to Know **84**

 The Inauguration: A Timeline **86**

 The Vice President: Duties & Selection **88**

 Next in Line: Presidential Succession at a Glance **90**

 All in a Day's Work **92**

 The Cabinet: What It Does and Who's in It **94**

 The First Lady **96**

 Impeachment: What? Why? When? How? **98**

 Keeping the Country Safe: National Security, Uncovered **100**

 The Civil Service **102**

1 MOVE-IN

The president-elect is not allowed into the White House—except as the current president's guest—until noon on January 20. Thus, the move-in needs to go like clockwork.

2 THE NEW FIRST FAMILY

The first family coordinates getting all its personal belongings to the White House.

PRESIDENTIAL TRANSITIONS:

EIGHT THINGS TO KNOW

Although nearly all US presidential elections are determined by the small hours of the Wednesday after Election Day, the new president's term doesn't start until January 20 of the following year.

3 NEW STAFF

As many as five hundred new staff members start with each new president, even if he or she is elected from the same party as the departing leader.

4 COORDINATION AND DÉCOR

Nothing is off limits when it comes to the West Wing décor. The president and administration can change everything—furnishings, paint, wallpaper, and more. The presidential staff coordinates cleaning, painting, carpeting, and choosing everything for the White House's offices and residential spaces.

5 NEW CHEF

The president can choose a new chef who will prepare meals for the family, starting with breakfast on January 21.

6 UPDATED GALLERY

The staff plans for updates that will happen at the time of inauguration. For instance, just outside the cabinet room is a gallery of photos of the president. It's updated right away with photos of the new leader's inauguration.

7 NEW WHEELS

The new president will travel in a brand-new limo. Each incoming president's limo is ordered ahead of time—by up to three years.

8 FUNERAL PLANS

Though it may seem macabre, the new president is asked to plan his (or her) funeral during the first week in office.

THE INAUGURATION

A TIMELINE

SWEARING-IN CEREMONIES

At the Capitol, the oath of office is administered—first to the vice president, and then to the president.

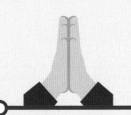

MORNING SERVICE

The tradition of attending a pre-ceremony worship service dates back to 1933.

PROCESSION

The outgoing president accompanies the incoming president to the Capitol.

THE OATH OF OFFICE

The president swears to "faithfully execute the office of president of the United States, and will to the best of my ability, preserve, protect, and defend the Constitution of the United States."

AN INAUGURATION MARKS THE PEACEFUL TRANSFER OF POWER BETWEEN THE OUTGOING AND INCOMING PRESIDENTS.

DEPARTURE

After the new president is sworn in, the departing president and first lady leave.

INAUGURAL ADDRESS

The new president gives a speech.

CELEBRATIONS

Immediately after the ceremony, the new president and guests attend a luncheon and inaugural parade. That evening, they—along with many distinguished guests—attend an inaugural ball.

DID YOU KNOW?

The first inaugural ball honored James and Dolly Madison and took place in 1809.

THE VICE PRESIDENT:

DUTIES & SELECTION

The vice president must be ready to assume the presidency in case of the death, resignation, or incapacitation of the current president.

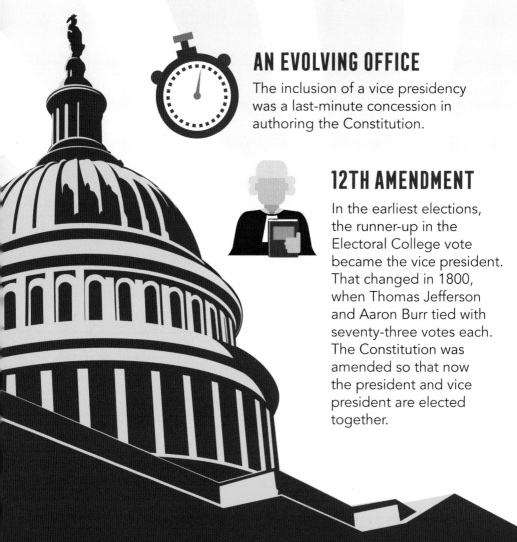

AN EVOLVING OFFICE

The inclusion of a vice presidency was a last-minute concession in authoring the Constitution.

12TH AMENDMENT

In the earliest elections, the runner-up in the Electoral College vote became the vice president. That changed in 1800, when Thomas Jefferson and Aaron Burr tied with seventy-three votes each. The Constitution was amended so that now the president and vice president are elected together.

VICE PRESIDENT
OFFICIAL DUTY

OFFICIAL DUTY

The vice president's only official duty—as outlined by the Constitution—is to preside over the Senate. The vice president is only allowed to vote in the Senate if there is a tie; thirty-six vice presidents have cast 268 votes to do this.

SELECTING A RUNNING MATE

Today, the presidential nominee of each party carefully considers a running mate who can bring certain qualities to the ticket. These qualities include experience or regional appeal that can help reach a wider audience of voters.

DID YOU KNOW?

Four presidents had no vice president: John Tyler, Millard Fillmore, Andrew Johnson, and Chester Arthur. Each of them succeeded presidents who died in office at a time when there was no constitutional provision for choosing a VP successor.

14

The number of vice presidents who have ascended to the presidency.

Nine were appointed due to the death or resignation of a president:

John Tyler

Millard Fillmore

Andrew Johnson

Chester Arthur

Theodore Roosevelt

Calvin Coolidge

Harry Truman

Lyndon B. Johnson

Gerald Ford

Five were elected after serving as VP:

John Adams

Thomas Jefferson

Martin Van Buren

Richard Nixon

George H.W. Bush

NEXT IN LINE

PRESIDENTIAL SUCCESSION

AT A GLANCE

THE CONSTITUTION ESTABLISHED:

"In Case of the Removal of the President from Office, or of his Death, Resignation, or Inability to discharge the Powers and Duties of the said Office, the Same shall devolve on the Vice President."

FIRST VP SUCCESSOR:

When President William Henry Harrison died in office in 1841, Vice President John Tyler behaved as "acting president." His approach created the precedent that the vice president is elevated to the office.

PRESIDENTIAL SUCCESSION ACT

Passed in 1947, this act established the official order of succession.

1. Vice President
2. Speaker of the House
3. Senate President Pro Tempore
4. Secretary of State
5. Secretary of the Treasury
6. Secretary of Defense
7. Attorney General
8. Secretary of the Interior
9. Secretary of Agriculture
10. Secretary of Commerce
11. Secretary of Labor
12. Secretary of Health and Human Services
13. Secretary of Housing and Urban Development
14. Secretary of Transportation
15. Secretary of Energy
16. Secretary of Education
17. Secretary of Veterans Affairs
18. Secretary of Homeland Security

DID YOU KNOW?

8 presidents have died while in office

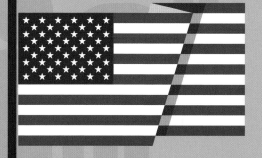

4 OF NATURAL CAUSES:

William Henry Harrison • 1841
Pneumonia (served only thirty days)

Zachary Taylor • 1850
Acute cholera or gastroenteritis

Warren G. Harding • 1923
Heart attack

Franklin Delano Roosevelt • 1945
Stroke

4 BY ASSASSINATION:

Abraham Lincoln • 1865
James Garfield • 1881
William McKinley • 1901
John F. Kennedy • 1963

ALL IN A DAY'S WORK

The president's day can be packed with meetings, events, briefings, speeches, and public ceremonies. A typical day may include:

Addressing the media

Meetings with members of Congress, cabinet members, or other advisers

Phone or in-person meetings with other heads of state

Security briefings from the FBI, CIA, NSA, or Department of Homeland Security

THE WHITE HOUSE

Built in 1800, the White House is where every president since John Adams has lived and worked.

For the entirety of the four-year term, the president is the president—twenty-four hours a day, seven days a week. The president can be called into action at a moment's notice, at any time of the day or night.

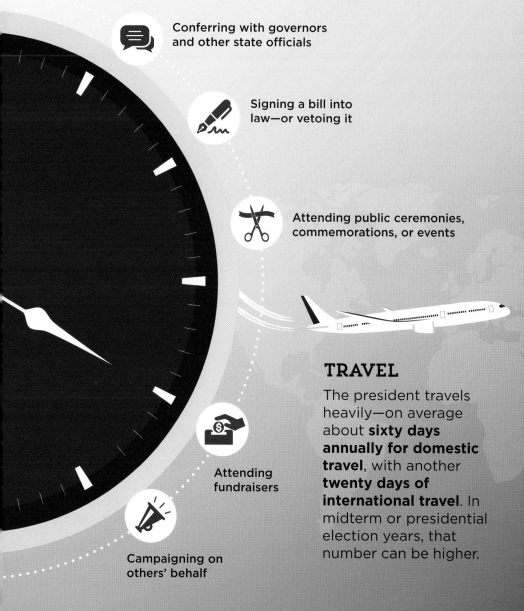

Conferring with governors and other state officials

Signing a bill into law—or vetoing it

Attending public ceremonies, commemorations, or events

Attending fundraisers

Campaigning on others' behalf

TRAVEL

The president travels heavily—on average about **sixty days annually for domestic travel**, with another **twenty days of international travel**. In midterm or presidential election years, that number can be higher.

THE CABINET

WHAT IT DOES AND WHO'S IN IT

A cabinet of **nonelected, appointed officials** advises the president.

DID YOU KNOW?

The American cabinet has its roots in the **English Parliament's "cabinet council,"** whose members once guided the monarch on political issues. We also call cabinet departments either **inner** (which means greater access to the president) or **outer** (less access to the president).

THE FIRST CABINET

Originally there were only four cabinet positions: **Department of State**, **Department of War** (now Defense), **Treasury Department**, and an **Attorney General**. George Washington believed his cabinet members should be policy advisers and department managers. In many ways, his administration set a precedent that has lasted until today.

CABINET SELECTION

Choosing cabinet members is one of the president-elect's first duties. The president-elect considers close friends, longtime allies, campaign loyalists, elected officials, and experts from the private sector. Through cabinet appointments, the president can also extend an olive branch to members of the opposite party.

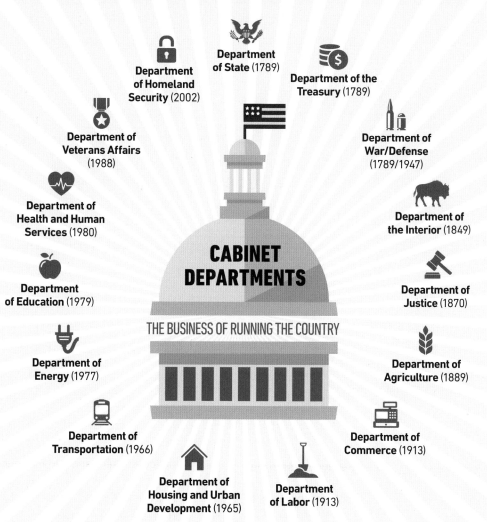

Department of State (1789)

Department of Homeland Security (2002)

Department of the Treasury (1789)

Department of Veterans Affairs (1988)

Department of War/Defense (1789/1947)

Department of Health and Human Services (1980)

Department of the Interior (1849)

CABINET DEPARTMENTS

Department of Education (1979)

Department of Justice (1870)

THE BUSINESS OF RUNNING THE COUNTRY

Department of Energy (1977)

Department of Agriculture (1889)

Department of Transportation (1966)

Department of Commerce (1913)

Department of Housing and Urban Development (1965)

Department of Labor (1913)

THE FIRST LADY

Although the Constitution never mentions the first lady, the role of the president's spouse has grown into an important and influential one. She usually champions a cause she is passionate about.

38

Number of first ladies who have occupied the White House.

6 Famous First Ladies
& Their Causes

Eleanor Roosevelt
1933–1945

Transformed the role from hostess to public advocate through her passion for activism and social service.

Jacqueline Kennedy
1961–1963

Restored the beauty and elegance of the White House and created the White House Historical Association.

Betty Ford
1974–1977

Fought against and raised awareness of substance abuse and founded the Betty Ford Center.

Nancy Reagan
1981–1989

Founded the "Just Say No" campaign to encourage young people to turn down alcohol and drugs.

Laura Bush
2001–2009

Championed literacy and took a leadership role in comforting families after the 9/11 attacks.

Michelle Obama
2009–2017

Focused on physical and mental health, especially for children, through reforming school lunch programs and increasing access to healthy food.

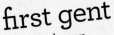

first gent
first gentleman
noun

What would a female president's spouse be called?

Speculation seems to favor "First Gent."

IMPEACHMENT

During his term, the president can leave office only through death, resignation, or impeachment.

WHAT IS IMPEACHMENT?

Impeachment is when the legislature brings charges against a government official for committing a crime, typically one they committed while in office. There is then a trial, and if convicted, the person will be removed from office.

POWER CHECK

The framers considered impeachment a potent tool to check power. Impeachment can be applied to the president as well as other federal officials.

WHY?

REASONS

The Constitution specifies **"Treason, Bribery or High Crimes and Misdemeanors"** but doesn't include more specifics on what these are.

WHEN?

2

IMPEACHED PRESIDENTS

Andrew Johnson, 1868
Bill Clinton, 1998

Both were acquitted by the Senate.

HOW?

THE HOUSE'S ROLE

Only the House of Representatives can determine grounds for impeachment. House members can introduce a bill or refer action to a committee. A majority of House representatives must vote "yes."

1

PRESIDENT RESIGNED

Richard Nixon, 1974

He left before likely impeachment proceedings could begin.

THE SENATE'S ROLE

The Senate conducts a trial of the impeached official, who can be convicted or acquitted.

99

KEEPING THE COUNTRY SAFE

NATIONAL SECURITY, UNCOVERED

The job of protecting the nation and its citizens falls to four security agencies.

FEDERAL BUREAU OF INVESTIGATION

▶ Mission of the FBI is to protect the American people and uphold the Constitution.

▶ Organized in 1908, the FBI has more than 400 regional offices across the country.

▶ Directors are limited to a single ten-year term because of the abuse of power by J. Edgar Hoover.

DID YOU KNOW?

During Prohibition, the FBI was very active in arresting notorious criminals like Al Capone and John Dillinger.

NATIONAL SECURITY AGENCY

▸ Developed during WWII and formally organized in 1952.

▸ Mission of the NSA is to monitor communication overseas and protect the US from cyberattacks.

▸ Surreptitiously collects electronic information about other countries.

CENTRAL INTELLIGENCE AGENCY

▸ Formally created in 1947 from WWII-era intelligence efforts.

▸ Mission of the CIA is to collect, analyze, and disseminate foreign intelligence to the president and other leaders of the US government.

▸ Only the president can direct the CIA to take a covert action.

DID YOU KNOW?

The CIA has been implicated in coups and assassinations worldwide, including in Syria, Iran, Guatemala, Indonesia, and Congo.

DEPARTMENT OF HOMELAND SECURITY

▸ Umbrella organization created after the 9/11 attacks.

▸ Includes the US Coast Guard, Secret Service, Transportation Security Administration, and more.

▸ Largest government reorganization since the Department of Defense.

THE CIVIL SERVICE

The federal bureaucracy includes the cabinet departments and three additional types of agencies: **independent executive agencies, independent regulatory commissions,** and **government corporations.** Together these are the civil service—or civilian workforce.

Government Corporations

These entities are created for commercial government activity and include:

» US Postal Service (USPS)

» Federal Deposit Insurance Corporation (FDIC)

» Amtrak (National Railroad Passenger Corporation)

Independent Executive Agencies

Reporting to the president, these agencies include, among others:

» Central Intelligence Agency (CIA)

» Small Business Administration (SBA)

» National Aeronautics and Space Administration (NASA)

» Peace Corps

Independent Regulatory Commissions

These were formed to regulate and enforce rules for certain sectors of the economy.

» Federal Communications Commission (FCC)

» US Consumer Product Safety Commission

» Securities and Exchange Commission

» Nuclear Regulatory Commission

1871 Year the civil service was established

Approximate number of civil service employees **2.8 MILLION** (according to the Office of Personnel Management)

CHAPTER 5

AMERICAN GOVERNMENT MADE LOCAL

 State Government:
An Overview **106**

 Local Matters:
County Government **108**

 Community Matters:
City Government **110**

 A Free Press: Media
& the Government **112**

 All About Interest
Groups: Wielding
Influence Large and
Small **114**

 The Lowdown
on Lobbyists **116**

 What You Can Do:
Entering the Political
Process **118**

 Power of
the People **120**

STATE GOVERNMENT

→ AN OVERVIEW ←

The US is a federalist government, which means that the federal and state governments share power, which creates a healthy tension. Here is how it all works.

FEDERAL vs. STATE POWERS

International Matters

National Defense

Education

Crime Control

Housing

Taxes

Exclusive Domain
Controlled exclusively by federal government

Shared Domain
Power is shared between federal and state governments

THE GOVERNOR

The governor is the highest elected state official, and he or she runs the state. Originally a position appointed by the king in colonial days, the governorship is today modeled after the presidency.

More than twenty governors have ascended to the vice presidency or presidency.

SAME SYSTEM, SMALLER SCALE

Each state has a constitution
and three branches of government—
legislative, executive, and judicial.
No two states are exactly alike, though.

STATE CONSTITUTIONS

State constitutions
are subordinate
to the "supreme
law of the land,"
which means
that provisions
that conflict with
federal law are
unconstitutional.

By the Numbers

Shortest:
Vermont
8,000 words

Longest:
Alabama
300,000 words

Strangest Provisions

California: specifies
the sizes of fruit boxes

Oklahoma:
states public
schools must
teach agriculture

LOCAL MATTERS:
COUNTY GOVERNMENT

County government is the most common jurisdiction of local government in most places in the US (with a few exceptions, as noted).

ORIGINS

Counties are modeled after the English shire of the Middle Ages. Each shire served as the administrative arm of the national government. When early American colonists arrived in the New World, they adopted this model.

3 TYPES

County government falls into three basic categories:

Commission, where a board carries out executive and legislative functions

Commission-administrator, where a board appoints an administrator

Council-executive, where an elected county executive serves as a chief administrator

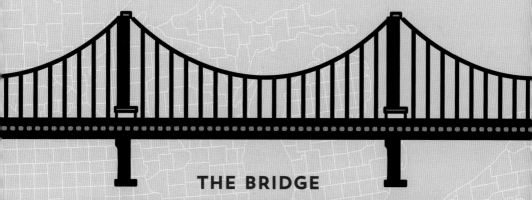

THE BRIDGE

County government serves as the bridge between state and local government. Its duties include, among others:

 Assessing and reassessing property values

 Keeping official records, such as birth, death, and marriage certificates

 Collecting taxes

 Maintaining roads and highways

 Constructing and maintaining municipal buildings

 Providing public assistance, such as food and welfare

EXCEPTIONS

Four states don't have county governments:

Alaska
has boroughs

Connecticut
abolished county governments in 1960

Louisiana
has parishes

Rhode Island
has no local government at the county level

COMMUNITY MATTERS:

CITY GOVERNMENT

When the US was founded, it consisted of rural communities. Today, the opposite is true: **nearly 80% of the population lives in or near a city of 50,000 or more residents**. And city government widely varies community to community.

INCORPORATION:

Incorporation means a city is a legally defined government entity, with powers delegated by state and county governments. Laws and regulations are approved by residents—voters. Cities then provide municipal services, such as transportation or refuse collection, to their residents.

FOUNDING

Cities are officially founded when a group of citizens creates a charter—the first step toward incorporation.

4 TYPES

Once incorporated, a city must choose a form of government from among four types:

1. **Mayor-council**—a mayor and a unicameral (one-chamber) council are elected.

2. **Council-manager**—an elected council appoints an administrator.

3. **Commission**—an elected commission performs city operations and oversees its agencies.

4. **New England town meeting**—voters decide annually on a budget, taxes, school spending, and other government matters. Only in use in Massachusetts, Connecticut, Vermont, Rhode Island, New Hampshire, and Maine.

CITY, TOWN, VILLAGE... WHAT'S IN A NAME?

In general, a city is larger than a town, and it has been officially incorporated. A town, village, or community may be unincorporated. Many cities provide services to unincorporated towns or communities in close proximity to one another.

CHARTER

Like a state constitution, a city charter defines the power and structure of its government.

MEDIA &
THE GOVERNMENT

The unrestricted flow of information, ideas, and opinions is critical to a true democracy. In the US, the media provides this flow at many levels, from national to local.

IST AMENDMENT
Guaranteed a free press as a **check on government power**

MEDIA INVESTIGATIONS
Investigations expose **corruption, influence, abuse,** and other activities that could have a negative effect on citizens and their freedoms.

WHAT'S NEWSWORTHY?

That depends. On a national level, hundreds of decisions and events take place daily in the three branches of government, so editors must decide on what to report. On a local level, the press may focus on what a national or state decision means for an area's residents.

A CHANGING LANDSCAPE

In colonial times, the media consisted of weekly newspapers. Today in the digital age, "the media" includes national, state, and local newspapers; content sites and aggregators; podcasts; TV networks; and more.

PRESS RESPONSIBILITIES

▸ Reporting on events and developments

▸ Investigating the institutions of government

▸ Promoting the exchange of ideas and opinions

▸ Endorsing national, state, and local candidates

SHAPING OPINION

Candidates are able to use the media to share their **stance on issues**, **make headlines**, and  **shape public opinion**. They do so through local events, press conferences, op-ed pieces and opinion columns, state or local political coverage, talk shows, social media, print media, election reporting, and more.

ALL ABOUT

INTEREST GROUPS

Wielding Influence Large and Small

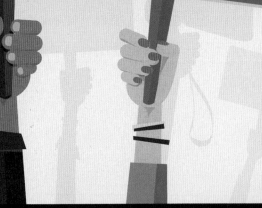

There are thousands of interest groups in the US. Formed by citizens for the purpose of asserting collective strength in the political process, these groups fall into three basic categories.

ECONOMIC INTEREST GROUPS
Protect or expand business priorities, such as labor unions, professional associations, and chambers of commerce

PUBLIC INTEREST GROUPS
Seek to protect citizens' rights and resources, such as civil liberties groups, environmental organizations, and local citizen-led organizations promoting community or social interests

ISSUE-DRIVEN GROUPS
Formed to focus on one particular issue, such as abortion-rights groups and gun-control organizations

The first **pro-independence** interest groups emerged in the 1770s.

American Medical Association

Americans for Prosperity

National Rifle Association

AARP (American Association of Retired Persons)

MOST PROMINENT

When measured in **dollars and followers**, these are some of the largest special interest groups in the US today.

MoveOn

US Chamber of Commerce

National Education Association

THE LOWDOWN ON LOBBYISTS

Since the earliest term of Congress, paid advocacy has influenced legislators in shaping public policy and making laws.

DID YOU KNOW?

Lobbyists outnumber members of Congress 23 to 1.

LOBBYING:

The process of seeking to influence legislators by making the priorities and opinions of your group known. Federal lobbyists are required to register with the Clerk of the United States House of Representatives and the Secretary of the United States Senate.

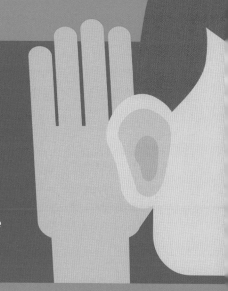

Lobbyists help provide direct access to key legislators, contributing vast networks and comprehensive knowledge of the political process to interest groups who hire them to:

- » Arrange meetings
- » Assist in drafting legislation
- » Testify in hearings
- » Organize protests
- » Host campaign fundraisers
- » Talk to the media
- » Run advertising campaigns
- » File lawsuits
- » And more

LOCAL, STATE, & FEDERAL LEVELS

Lobbying influences government at every level, from local to federal.

THE REVOLVING DOOR

Many former lawmakers become lobbyists, putting their extensive networks to use after their time in office ends.

WHAT YOU CAN DO

ENTERING THE POLITICAL PROCESS

For many private citizens, pursuing elected office in a local government is the starting point for entry into the political process.

OPEN TO EVERYONE

The founding fathers created a government system that today is **open to participation by all**—not just career politicians and civil servants. Many local officials work full-time jobs in addition to serving in their local governments.

DID YOU KNOW?

Volunteering for a local candidate's campaign can provide valuable experience for first-timers prior to running for office.

REASONS AND MOTIVATIONS

Many local politicians and aspirants seek office because of:

- ▸ Their drive to inspire others
- ▸ A commitment to public service
- ▸ A desire to change the status quo
- ▸ The wish to gain experience to seek higher office

ENTRY POINTS

Entry-level political offices give citizens a foothold and valuable experience. These offices can include:

- ▸ Library trustee
- ▸ Village board or town council
- ▸ School board
- ▸ County-level elected office, such as a freeholder or selectman

GETTING STARTED

Seeking any office requires a base of support. While local regulations vary from town to town and county to county, many positions require a petition with a certain number of signatures to even appear on the ballot. Candidates can find more information on what they need to get started at **www.runforoffice.org**.

· POWER ·

OF THE
PEOPLE

Prominent Protests
and Demonstrations

**Bonus Army
March on
Washington**
1932

**March on Washington
for Jobs and Freedom**
1963

**Million Man
March**
1995

The 1st Amendment protects citizens' right to organize in support of, or opposition to, changes to laws and policies. Because the country's founders had created a nation in opposition to British rule, **the right to freedom of speech and assembly—indeed, the fundamental right to dissent—formed an essential cornerstone of the Constitution.**

Opposition in many forms

Opposition to laws and policies can take many forms, including **grassroots movements**, **community organizing**, **mobilizing**, and **formal protests**.

Occupy Wall Street

2011

Women's March

2017

Did You Know?

The Women's March was the largest single-day protest in history.

INDEX

A

Adams, John, 89
Adams, John Quincy, 81
Adams, Samuel, 28
Amendments to Constitution
  1st Amendment, 37, 39, 112, 121
  12th Amendment, 88
  19th Amendment, 61
  22nd Amendment, 75
  24th Amendment, 61
  26th Amendment, 61
  about, 34–37
  Bill of Rights (freedoms secured by), 35–37
  definition of, 35
  number of, 35, 45
  proposal and ratification process, 35, 44
  superseding court rulings, 45
American government. See also American Revolution; Constitution; Founding of American government
  about: overview of this book and, 11
  entering the political process, 118–19
  interest groups and, 114–15
  lobbying, 116–17
American Revolution
  Continental Congress and, 21, 22, 24
  Declaration of Independence and, 22–23
  events leading up to, 18–20
  first armed conflicts, 21
  how it happened, 20–21
  taxation issues and, 18–19
  timeline of, 24–25
  what it was about, 20
Anatomy of American government. See also Executive branch (president and administration); Judicial branch (courts); Legislative branch (Congress); President references
  branches in action, 44–45
  checks and balances, 44–45
  three branches of government, 42–43
Arms, right to bear, 37
Arnold, Gen. Benedict, 24
Articles of Confederation, 26–27
Assembly, right to petition and, 36, 120–21

B

Baron de Montesquieu, 15, 45
Bill of Rights, American, 35–37
Bill of Rights, English, 15
Blue states, red states, swing states, 70–71
Boston Tea Party, 20
Branches of government, 42–43. See also President references; specific branches
Bush, George H.W., 89
Bush, George W., 81
Bush, Laura, 97

C

Cabinet, 94–95
Central Intelligence Agency (CIA), 101, 103
Charters, 111
Checks and balances, 44–45
City government, 110–11
Civil service (civilian workforce), 102–3
Colonies
  early arrivals and settlements, 17
  Era of Salutary Neglect, 19
  home rule of, 17, 21
  original thirteen, 16–17
  taxes creating resentment and rebellion, 18–19. See also American Revolution

Commission, as city government, 111
Common Sense (Paine), 21, 24
Congress. *See* Legislative branch
  (Congress)
Constitution
    amendments. *See* Amendments to
      Constitution
    Articles 1 to 6, 30–31
    Bill of Rights, 35–37
    cornerstone freedoms, 36–37
    drafting of, 29
    presidential succession and, 90–91
    ratification of, 32–33
    right to petition and assembly, 36
    separation of church and state and,
      38–39
Constitutions, state, 107
Continental Congress, 21, 22, 24
Cornwallis, Gen. Charles, 24
Corporations, government, 103
Council-manager city government, 111
County government (origins, types,
  and functions), 108–9
Currency Act (1764), 19

D

Dawes, William, 24
Declaration of Independence, 22–23
Declaration of Rights, 21
Democratic Party history, 64–65
Democratic-Republican Party, 65
Department of Homeland Security, 101
Documents influencing America, 15

E

Elections and voting, 59–81. *See also*
  President, electing
    amendments related to, 61
    ballot access, 63
    conservatives and liberals, 71
    cost of running for office, 63
    Democratic Party history, 64–65

election day, 62, 72–73
entering the political process, 118–19
facts about voting, 60–61
midterms, 62
nominations, 63
outcome determination, 73
red states, blue states, swing states,
  70–71
registering to vote, 61
Republican Party history, 66–67
term limits and, 74–75
third parties and independents,
  68–69
turnout and voter polling, 73
two-party history, 69
volunteering, 118
English Bill of Rights, 15
Era of Salutary Neglect, 19
Executive branch (president and
  administration). *See also* President,
  electing; President and administration leadership
    appointees approved by Senate, 47
    checks and balances and, 44–45
    functions and responsibilities, 43,
      44, 92–93
    presidential roles and eligibility, 57
    senators elected as president, 42

F

Federal Bureau of Investigation (FBI),
  100
Federalists vs. Anti-Federalists, 28–29
Fillmore, Millard, 89
First Continental Congress, 21
First lady, 96–97
Ford, Betty, 97
Ford, Gerald, 89
Founding of American government.
  See also American Revolution; Con-
  stitution
    Articles of Confederation and, 26–27
    documents influencing, 15

the Enlightenment (Age of Reason) and, 14–15
Federalists vs. Anti-Federalists, 28–29
ideas and ideals behind, 14
prominent thinkers behind, 15
resentment and rebellion, 18–19
thirteen colonies and, 16–17
transitional government, 26–27
Founding of cities, 110
Fourth of July, 23
Funeral plans for president, 85

G

Garfield, James, 91
Gerrymandering, 63
GOP (Grand Old Party), 67
Governors, state, 106
Green Party, 69
Gubernatorial term limits, 75

H

Hamilton, Alexander, 28, 29
Harding, Warren G., 91
Harrison, William Henry, 90, 91
Hayes, Rutherford B., 81
Henry, Partrick, 28
Hobbes, Thomas, 15
Homeland Security, Department of, 101
Home rule, 17, 21
House of Representatives. See Legislative branch (Congress)

I

Impeachment, 98–99
Incorporation of cities, 110
Independence Day, 23
Independent regulatory commissions, 103
Independents and third parties, 68–69
Interest groups and lobbying, 114–17

J

Jay, John, 28, 29
Jefferson, Thomas, 22, 39, 64, 75, 88, 89
Johnson, Andrew, 89, 99
Judicial branch (courts)
    checks and balances and, 44–45
    court of last resort, 55
    federal and state courts, 54–55
    functions and responsibilities, 43, 44
    history and powers, 53, 54–55
    judicial review, 55
    number of justices and judges, 55
    Supreme Court, 43, 52–53

K

Kennedy, Jacqueline, 97
Kennedy, John F., 91

L

Legislative branch (Congress)
    checks and balances and, 44–45
    cost of running for office, 63
    eligibility requirements, 47, 49
    functions and responsibilities, 42, 44
    House of Representatives, 42, 48–49
    impeachment and, 98–99
    lobbying influences, 116–17
    number of senators and representatives, 46, 49
    rules and committees of the House, 48
    Senate and senators, 42, 46–47
    special powers, 47, 48
    steps in building a law, 50–51
    term lengths, 46, 49
    term limits, 75
    tie-breaker in the Senate, 47
Libertarian Party, 69
Lincoln, Abraham, 66, 91
Lobbying, interest groups and, 114–17
Locke, John, 15, 39

M

Madison, James, 28, 29, 87
Marches and protests, 120–21
Mayflower Compact, 15
Mayor-council city government, 111
McKinley, William, 91
Media and government
    changing landscape, 113
    First Amendment and, 112, 121
    interest groups, lobbying and, 114–17
    investigations, 112
    newsworthy information, 112
    responsibilities of the press, 113
    shaping opinion, 113
Monroe, James, 28
Montgomery, Gen. Richard, 24

N

National security, 100–101
National Security Agency (NSA), 101
New England town hall government, 111
Nixon, Richard, 89, 99

O

Obama, Michelle, 97
Opposing government issues, 120–21

P

Paine, Thomas, 21, 24
Petition, right to assembly and, 36, 120–21
Petition of Right, 15
Political process, entering, 118–19
President, electing
    campaign organization and fundraising, 76
    debates and forums, 77
    election cycle, 62, 76
    Electoral College and, 78–81
    losing popular vote but winning Electoral College, 80–81
    nominations and elections, 63, 76–81
    primaries and caucuses, 77
    selecting running mate, 89
    term limits, 57, 74–75
    tie-breaker, 80
President and administration leadership, 83–103. See also Executive branch (president and administration)
    assassinated presidents, 91
    cabinet, 94–95
    civil service (civilian workforce), 102–3
    first lady, 96–97
    funeral plans for president, 85
    government corporations, 103
    impeachment, 98–99
    inauguration timeline, 86–87
    independent executive agencies, 103
    line of succession, 90–91
    national security, 100–101
    new things for new president, 84–85
    presidents who died in office, 91
    transition to new president and staff, 84–85
    Twelfth Amendment and, 88
    typical day, illustrated, 92–93
    vice president duties and selection, 88–89
    vice presidents who ascended to presidency, 89
Presidential Succession Act, 91
Press, freedom of speech and, 37. See also Media and government
Protests and demonstrations, 120–21

Q

Quartering Act (1765), 19

R

Reagan, Nancy, 97
Red states, blue states, swing states, 70–71

Reform Party, 69
Regulatory commissions, independent, 103
Religion
    freedom of, 36
    separation of church and state, 38–39
Republican Party history, 66–67
Revere, Paul, 24
Roosevelt, Eleanor, 97
Roosevelt, Franklin Delano, 75, 91

S

Secondat, Charles de (Baron de Montesquieu), 15, 45
Second Continental Congress, 22, 24
Security, national, 100–101
Senate. *See* Legislative branch (Congress)
Speech, freedom of the press and, 37
Stamp Act (1765), 19
State and local government
    bridge between, 109
    charters, 111
    cities, towns, villages, and communities compared, 111
    city government formation and types, 110–11
    county government (origins, types, and functions), 108–9
    entering the political process, 118–19
    lobbying influences, 117
    state constitutions, 107
    state government overview, 106–7
    states without county governments, 109
    term limits, 75
Succession, presidential, 90–91
Sugar Act (1764), 19
Swing states, red states, blue states, 70–71

T

Taxes
    boycotts and rising tensions from, 18–19
    British laws enacted to raise, 19
    no taxation without representation, 18
    resentment of, 18–19
Taylor, Zachary, 91
Term limits, 57, 74–75
Third parties and independents, 68–69
Thirteen colonies, 16–17
Tiebreaker for presidential elections, 80
Tiebreaker for Senate votes, 47
Townshend Acts (1767), 19
Trump, Donald J., 81
Tyler, John, 89, 90

V

Van Buren, Martin, 89
Vetoes, 44, 51
Vice president duties and selection, 88–89
Vice president(s)
    amendment changing election of, 88
    duties and selection, 88–89
    presidential succession and, 90–91
    presidents serving without, 89
    selected as running mates, 89
    who ascended to presidency, 89
Volunteering, 118–19

W

Washington, George, 24, 56, 57, 75, 94

ABOUT THE DESIGNER

Carissa Lytle is a marketer-turned-designer who loves creating infographics because of the way they beautifully meld typography, illustration, and design. She studied marketing at DePaul University and visual communication design at the School of the Art Institute of Chicago before starting out on her own as a freelance designer. Fast-forward fifteen years and she now owns the award-winning, full-service design firm Right Angle Studio. Alongside her husband, Patrick—a former CMO with a similar entrepreneurial spirit—the pair balance creative insight and marketing know-how to run their business like a well-oiled machine. When they aren't collaborating on their clients' latest projects, you can find them enjoying their free time with their children on Chicago's North Shore.

ABOUT THE AUTHOR

Jara Kern tapped her entrepreneurial streak as a kindergartner, when she wrote to Hasbro with the idea for a new line of My Little Pony toys, accompanied by names, marketing copy, and detailed illustrations. While she's moved on from My Little Ponies, her knack for organizing ideas and expressing them in sparkling copy has stayed with her—and helped her nurture a thriving career. When she's not strategizing or writing, you'll find her running trails or learning about birds and bugs with her three children. She holds a degree in music performance from the Oberlin Conservatory of Music and an MBA from the University of Wisconsin-Madison.

GET GRAPHIC!

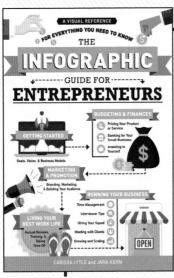

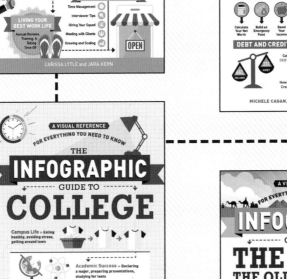

adamsmedia
An Imprint of Simon & Schuster
A CBS COMPANY

PICK UP OR DOWNLOAD YOUR COPIES TODAY!